North Carolina Midland Railroad Co.

Collation of Charters, Amendments, and Consolidations

March 10, 1891

North Carolina Midland Railroad Co.

Collation of Charters, Amendments, and Consolidations
March 10, 1891

ISBN/EAN: 9783337815363

Printed in Europe, USA, Canada, Australia, Japan

Cover: Foto ©Andreas Hilbeck / pixelio.de

More available books at **www.hansebooks.com**

ORTH CAROLINA MIDLAND

RAILROAD COMPANY.

COLLATION OF

HARTERS, AMENDMENTS,

AND CONSOLIDATIONS.

MARCH 10th, 1891.

GREENSBORO:
Reece & Elam, Book and Job Printers.
1891.

ARTICLES OF ASSOCIATION

OF THE

WINSTON, SALEM AND MOORESVILLE R. R. CO.

AUGUST 6TH, 1878.

We the undersigned agree to form ourselves into a company for the purpose of constructing, maintaining and operating a Railroad for public use in the conveyance of persons and property:

And for that purpose, in pursuance of an act of the General Assembly ratified on the 8th of Feb. 1872, (which see) do make and sign the following articles of Association, to-wit:

I. Said Company is named and styled "The Winston Salem and Mooresville Railroad Company."'

II. Said Railroad shall continue to exist for the term of Ninety Years.

III. Said Railroad shall run from Winston or Salem, in the county of Forsyth, through the counties of Davidson or Yadkin, Davie and Rowan to Mooresville, in the county of Iredell, a distance of sixty miles, and said Road is to touch the corporate limits of the town of Mocksville.

The capital stock of said company shall be Three Hundred and Fifty Thousand Dollars, divided into Three Thousand and Five Hundred shares of One Hundred dollars each. The following are the names of the six Directors of said company, who shall manage it's affairs for the first year, and until others are chosen; Also with their places of residence:

W. C. Wilson..........................Farmington, N. C.
A. M. Booe...........................Mocksville, N. C.
S. A, Lourance........................Back Creek, N. C.

Isaac Harris..Mooresville, N. C.
S. E. Allen..Winston, N. C.
C. H. Wiley...   "   "

We the undersigned agree to take the shares of the capital stock in said company set opposite our names, and, pay therefor at such times and in such installments as may be required by the directors of said Company.

J. R. McCorkle..................... .....Mooresville, One Share.
A. Leazar..............................   "   " .   "
I. H. Stockton, (By G. W. Hinshaw, Prox.)Winston,   "   "
S. E. Allen...........................   "   .. "
James O. Moore...'....................Mooresville' "   "
J. A. Bitting......................... Winston,   "   "
Isaac Harris..................... ...Mooresville, Ten   "
A. M. Booe........................... Mocksville, Eight "
W. C. Wilson.........................Farmington, One   "
H. B. Howard........................·............Mocksville, Five "·
Jas. L. Adams,.......................   "   One   "
R. L. Goodman....... ....Mooresville, Five   "
W. A. Lucky...................... Third Creek, One   "
C. C. Krider......................... Mt. Vernon, "   "
F. M. Johnson........................ Farmington, "   "
D. D. Johnson...................•...... Wood Leaf, Two   "
L. A. Furches........................ Farmington, One   "
S. A. Lourance.......................Back Creek, Ten   "
S. C. Rankin.........................   "   Five   "
B. A. Knox...........................Third Creek, One   "
T. B. Bailey...:.....................Mocksville,   "   "
R. D. Brown.........................Winston,   "   "
W. L. Brown.........................   "   "   "
J. C. Conrad........................Huntsville,   "   "
L. C. Laugenour.....................Louisville,   "   "
C. H. Wiley........................Winston,   "   "

NORTH CAROLINA:

Before me personally appeared W. C. Wilson, A. M. Booe, S. A. Lourance, C. H. Wiley, Isaac Harris and S. E. Allen, who after being duly sworn say that they are three or more of the Directors named in the articles of Association entered into by the subscribers therein named for the purpose of construction, maintaining and operating a Narrow Guage Railroad from Winston, Salem to Mooresville in the county of Iredell. That at least One Thousand of the stock for every mile of Railroad proposed to be made between the points aforesaid, have been subscribed thereto and five per cent paid thereon in good faith and in cash, to the Directors named in articles of Association.

They further state that it is intended in good faith to construct maintain and operate the Road mentioned in said articles of Association.

W. C. WILSON,
A. M. BOOE,
S. A. LOURANCE,
ISAAC HARRIS,
S. E. ALLEN,
C. H. WILEY.

Sworn to and subscribed before me, this 30th day of July, 1878.

H. B. HOWARD,

[SEAL OF OFFICE.]   *Clerk Superior Court of Davie County.*

STATE OF NORTH CAROLINA, }
OFFICE SECRETARY OF STATE. }

RALEIGH, August 6th, 1878.

I, J. A. Englehard, Secretary of State, certify the foregoing to be a true copy of the Articles of Association of the Winston, Salem and Mooresville Railroad Company, filed and recorded in this office in pursuance of chap. 99, sec. 2, Battle's Revisal.

Witness my hand and seal of Office the 6th day of August, 1878.

JOS. A. ENGLEHARD.
Secretary of State.

At a meeting of the Directors of the Winston-Salem and Mooresville Narrow Guage Railroad Company, held at Mocksville, N. C., July 30th, 1878. there were present, Messrs. W. C. Wilson, Chairman, S. E. Allen, Isaac Harris, S. L. Lourance, C. H. Wiley and A. M. Booe.

On motion Mr. S. E. Allen the secretary was instructed to buy a book for the use of said Railroad Company. It being ascertained that at least One Thousand Dollars per mile had been subscribed, and (5%) five per cent thereon paid to said Directors: It was resolved that the necessary certificate be made to the Secretary of State for a grant of charter under the general Railroad Laws. On motion of Mr. Harris Capt. A. M. Booe was delegated to make application in person to the Hon. Secretary of State. On motion of Mr. C. H. Wiley, there was a committe of three appointed to correspond with several Engineers and Surveyors for the purpose of getting propositions for surveying and locating the road. The Chairman appointed the following gentlemen, C. H. Wiley, · Isaac Harris, A. M. Booe and S. E. Allen. On motion, Messrs. C. H. Wiley and S. E. Allen were appointed a committee to get up By-Laws and Articles on the road for publication. On motion of Mr. Harris the meeting adjourned to meet at Mooresville on Aug. 21st, '78.

W. C. WILSON, Chm'n.
R. D. BROWN, Sec'y.

WINSTON, N. C., October 20th, 1880.

At a meeting of the Stockholders of the Winston, Salem and Mooresville Railroad Company, held this day in the Court House at Winston, pursuant to a call by the board of Directors of said road,

Mr. A. Leazar was elected chairman, and R. D. Brown, secretary.

It was announced by the chair that the object of the

meeting was to consider and take action upon the articles of consolidation previously adopted by the directors of the Winston, Salem and Mooresville Railroad, the Winston, Salem and Madison Railroad and the Dan Valley and Yadkin River Railroad, at joint meeting held at the office of Hon. T. J. Wilson in the town of Winston on the 9th day of Sept. 1880.

On motion Messrs. W. C. Wilson and R. D. Brown were appointed a committee to examine credentials and verify proxies, and the committee reported that 492¼ shares were represented either in person or by proxy, the same being more than ⅔ of the stock subscribed.

Upon further motion this report was accepted and the committee discharged.

On motion of Capt. J. O. Moore, the articles of consolidation of the several above named roads were submitted to the meeting for ratification or rejection. And a vote being had by ballot, 492¼ shares were recorded in favor of "ratification," and it was announced by the chair that the action of the joint meeting of the Directors aforesaid was unanimously endorsed.

Upon motion of Col. J. W. Alspaugh, the secretary was requested to prepare and forward to the Secretary of State, a copy of the proceedings of this meeting.

On motion it was: *Resolved*, That Mrs. J. L. Adams, widow of J. L. Adams, deceased, and late of the firm of Sanford & Adams, be and she is hereby released from the payment of one half of the subsciption made by her late husband to the Winston, Salem and Mooresville Railroad Company.

It was ordered that the Secretary of the Winston, Salem and Mooresville Railroad Company, deliver all books, papers and other valuables in his possession belonging to the Winston, Salem and Mooresville Railroad

Company, to the secretary of the consolidated company.
And thereupon, no further business coming before the
meeting, adjournment was had *sine die*.

R. D. BROWN, Sec.

PROCEEDINGS OF A JOINT MEETING of the Directors, of the
Winston; Salem and Mooresville Railroad; the Winston, Salem
and Madison Railroad, and the Dan River and Yadkin Valley
Railroad Companies, held in Judge T. J. Wilson's office, in
the town of Winston, N. C., Sept. 9th, 1880.

Present on part of Winston, Salem and Mooresville
Railroad Company, Messrs. W. C. Wilson, C. H. Wiley,
S. A. Lourance, Isaac Harris and S. E. Allen. On part
of the Winston, Salem and Madison Railroad Company,
Messrs. J. F. Shaffner, J. E. Gilmer, P. W. Hairston and
J. W. Fries, and on the part of the Dan Valley and Yad-
kin River Railroad Company, Messrs. J. T. Morehead,
Joseph Vaughn, E. W. Anderson and P. W. Hairston.

On motion of Rev. W. C. Wilson, Dr. J. F. Shaffner
called to the chair, and S. E. Allen made secretary
of the meeting.

On motion of Col. J. T. Morehead, the Articles of Consolidated Association, as submitted by Messrs. Wilson
and Clement was taken up by sections, and after due dis-
cussion and consideration of each section were unanious-
ly adopted as a whole, as follows:

AGREEMENT AND ARTICLES OF ASSOCIATION.

Know all men by these presents, that the Railroad
corporations named below, to wit: The Dan Valley and
Yadkin River Railroad Company, the Winston, Salem
and Madison Railroad Company, and the Winston, Salem
and Mooresville Railroad Company, Railroad Companies duly incorporated under the laws of the State of
North Carolina—in pursuance of an act of the General

Assembly of North Carolina, entitled " Railroad Companies," and appearing in Battle's Revisal, Chapter 99, Sections 58, 59, 60 and 61, do make and enter into this joint agreement by and with each other, to merge and consolidate the Capital Stock, franchises and property of the three several corporations above named, so as to form and establish one Railway corporation for the purpose of constructing, maintaining and operating a continious line of Railroad for public use in the conveyance of persons and property from a point on the Virginia State line in Rockingham County, North Carolina, east of Smith River, by the way of Madison in the county of Rockingham, thence passing through the county of Stokes and by the way of the town of Winston in the county of Forsyth, and by the way of Mocksville in the county of Davie, thence through the county of Rowan to the town of Mooresville, in the county of Iredell.

I. The corporate name of said Company thus formed shall be " The North Carolina Midland Railroad Company."

II. Said Company is to continue in existence as a corporation for the period of Ninety-six (96) years.

III. That said Railroad shall be constructed, maintained and operated between the termini and along the route as described above, and the line of Railroad contemplated and herein provided for shall be constructed with all proper turnouts, sidings, depot buildings and all other appurtenances of a Railway.

IV. The amount of the Capital Stock of said Company shall be One Million and a half dollars, consisting of Fifteen thousand shares of One hundred dollars each.

V. There shall be a President, Vice-President, Secretary and Treasurer, and nine Directors of the Company; the Directors to be annually elected by a stock vote of the Company, and the other officers annually by the Directors. The other employees shall be selected as the By-Laws shall direct. The Annual meeting of the said Company shall be on the first Thursday of July in each and every year, and the first annual meeting shall be held in the town of Winston, N. C. on the first Thursday in July 1881, and the following persons shall constitute the Board of Directors and officers of said Company, to wit:

A. Leazar of Mooresville, A. M. Booe of Mocksville, W. C. Wilson, Mocksville, J. E. Gilmer and C. H. Wiley of Winston, J. W. Fries of Salem, P. W. Hairston of Sauratown, L. W. Anderson and J. M. Vaughn of Madison, as Directors.

John S. Barham of Alexandria, Va., President; J. T. Morehead of Leaksville, Vice-President, and J. W. Alspaugh of Winston, Secretary and Treasurer.

VI. Subscribers to the stock of either of the companies shall have the same standing and rights in the consolidated Company as regards payments and assessments as they now have in their respective companies.

VII. It is hereby further stipulated that this joint agreement of consolidation shall be submitted to the stockholders of each of the corporations, parties to this agreement at a meeting thereof called separately for the purpose of taking the same into consideration; due notice of the time and place of holding said meetings, and the object thereof shall be given as prescribed by section 59, sub-section 2 of the act above referred to, and if two thirds of all the votes of all the stockholders, shall be for the adoption of said agreement, then that fact shall be certified thereon by the secretaries of the respective Companies under the seals thereof, and the agreement so adopted, or a certified copy thereof shall be filed in the office of the Secretary of State.

In testimony of the above agreement the Directors of the several Corporations above named have hereunto subscribed their names and attached the corporate seals of their respective Companies. Dated at Winston, N. C., the 9th day of September, A. D., 1880.

[SIGNED]

W. C. WILSON,
C. H. WILEY,
ISAAC HARRIS,
S. A. LOURANCE,
S. E. ALLEN,

Directors Winston, Salem and Mooresville Railroad Co.

P. W. HAIRSTON,
J. W. FRIES,
J. E. GILMER,
J. F. SHAFFNER,

Directors Winston, Salem and Madison Railroad Co,

J. TURNER MOREHEAD,
L. W. ANDERSON,
P. W. HAIRSTON,
J. M. VAUGHN,

Directors Dan Valley and Yadkin River Railroad Co.

On motion of C. H. Wiley the President and Secretary was requested to notify Jno. S. Barham of his election, and ask his acceptance.

On motion of J. W. Fries a seal of this Company was adopted.

The undersigned Secretary of the Winston, Salem and Madison Railroad Company, hereby certifies that at a meeting of the stockholders of said company held in the town of Winston, on Wednesday, the 20th day of October, A. D., 1880, after due notice to said stockholders when and where—on a vote by ballot taken, said agreement and articles of association were adopted by stock votes, the same being two thirds of all the votes of all the stockholders of said Company.

In testimony whereof he has hereunto subscribed his name and attached the seal of said Company.

....

Secretary and Treasurer.

DIRECTORS MEETING.

WINSTON, N. C., Feb. 24, 1881.

At a meeting of the Directors of the North Carolina Midland Railroad Company, held in the town of Winston, on the 24th day of February, 1881, the following Directors were present, and participated in the meeting, to-wit:

J. T. Morehead, Vice-President, C. H. Wiley, J. E. Gilmer, J. W. Fries, T. J. Wilson and A. M. Booe.

On motion by Mr. Wiley, the Vice President, was called to the chair.

On motion the following resolutions were adopted:

I. That the Vice-President, J. T. Morehead be authorized to discontinue or continue at his discretion, the work of construction of the road.

II. That the Hon. J. S. Barbour, President of the Company and J. Turner Morehead, Vice-President, and each of them separately be authorized to open books of subscription to this road, and also to solicit and receive propositions for its construction, and that they be requested to report to the next monthly meeting of this Board.

III. On motion the Secretary and Treasurer was instructed out of any funds in his hands to reimburse himself for having paid $25.00 to the State, the same being tax on the amendment made by the Legislature, to the charter of this Road.

IV. On motion the meeting adjourned to meet on the 24th day of March at Winston, unless earlier called together.

President.

J. W. ALSPAUGH,
Secretary.

The President then stated that in accordance with the resolution he, on behalf of the Virginia Midland Railroad Company, would appropriate Fifty Thousand Dollars to the North Carolina Midland Railroad Company, and take the first Mortgage Bonds of the North Carolina Midland Railroad Company hereafter to be issued for an equal amount in payment of that appropriation.

On motion by Mr. Hairston the above appropriation by the Virginia Midland Railroad Company was accepted by the Board, and the thanks of the Company tendered to the Virginia Midland Railroad for the same.

On motion it was further resolved that the President of this Company be and is hereby authorized to expend in the construction of the road the amount of the above appropriation, and the sums obtained from individual and corporate subscriptions to the stock of the company, whether such subscriptions be in money, labor or material, and that he be and is hereby authorized to begin the construction by contract or otherwise at such points on the line as he may deem most expedient and advisable; Provided, however, that the amounts called for on the subscriptions to the company be expended in the sections where the subscriptions were made.

Resolved further, that the local Directors from the various counties and towns which have authorized subscriptions to the stock of the company be requested to urge upon the said county and municipal authorities the necessity of immediately making the formal subscriptions which have been authorized in accordance with law.

Resolved, that the Treasurer of the company be directed to call for the payment of all the individual subscriptions to the stock which have been already made or which may hereafter be made, in monthly installments of 10 per cent, and that the Treasurer be and is hereby authorized to take the proper steps to collect such installments of 10 per cent for each month.

Resolved, that the Treasurer be and is hereby directed to call for and receive from the county and municipal authorities, the bonds which have been or may be authorized to be raised in payment of the several county, town and township subscriptions in bonds; but when such authorities determine to pay the subscriptions in cash, then the Treasurer is directed to collect the installments in the same manner as the installments on the individual subscriptions.

Resolved, that the Treasurer of this Company be and is hereby authorized to accept the formal subscriptions to the stock to be made by any county, town or township authorities, and said subscriptions shall be made in the presence of the Treasurer and one or more of the Directors.

Resolved, that the resolution of the meeting of this Board of Feb. 24, 1881, authorizing the President and the Vice-President to open books of subscription be rescinded.

Resolved, that the President be authorized to have such surveys made as he may deem advisable and prudent, looking towards a southern extension.

These surveys are at the request of sundry delegations from points in the State of South Carolina, and will be mainly at the expense of the sections through which they are made.

On motion, it was ordered that the Treasurer purchase a suitable seal for the Company.

On motion, it was ordered that the Secretaries and Treasurers of those Companies which were consolidated into this Company, be requested to hand over the Records, Books and papers, together with all matters relating thereto, to the Secretary and Treasurer of this Company.

On motion, it was ordered that if it be found necessary the Secretary and Treasurer may employ one or more persons to aid him in the collection of assessments on stock ordered by the meetings, on such terms as he may deem proper.

On motion, it was resolved that the Engineer in charge of construction be authorized to receive subscriptions to the Capital stock, payable in material or labor.

On motion, the President and Vice-President of this company were appointed a committee to draw up a set of By-Laws for the government of this company, and that they report at the next meeting of this Board.

On motion, J. W. Fries, J. E. Gilmer and C. H. Wiley were appointed a committee on accounts.

On motion, the Secretary and Treasurer was allowed a salary of $600, and that he give his individual Bond for the faithful performance of his duty, in the sum of Ten Thousand Dollars.

On motion, it was resolved that Col. J. B. Yates be continued as chief Engineer, at the same compensation as heretofore.

On motion, the board now adjourned, subject to the call of the President.

President.

J. W. ALSPAUGH,
Secretary.

STOCKHOLDFR'S MEETING, AUG. 24, 1882.

The Stockholders of the North Carolina Midland Railroad Company in general meeting assembled, pursuant to notice, at Winston, North Carolina, Aug. 24, 1882, adopt the following resolutions:

I. That power and authority is hereby granted to and invested in the Board of Directors of this company to lease the rights, property and franchises thereof to the Virginia Midland Railway Company for a term not exdeeding forty years from the date hereof; said lease shall include the real and personal property of said Company, its franchises, corporate rights and privileges and sidings, depots, shops, houses, bridges, and other works and property whether constructed or to be constructed, and whether now in possession, or hereafter to be acquired.

The consideration for said lease shall be the payment to this company or to whomsoever it may designate by the said Virginia Midland Railroad Company of an annual rental of One hundred and twenty thousand Dollars, during the term of this lease, and the further consideration of the annual payment by the Virginia Midland Railway Company, of all proper expenses of maintaining the organization of the North Carolina Midland Railroad during the term of said lease, provided, said payments shall not exceed $2,000.00 per annum. With the limitations above set forth, the date, terms, conditions and details of said lease shall be such as may be determined and agreed upon by the Board of Directors of this Company. In making said lease, authority is granted to the said Board of Directors to covenant that the said Road shall be completed throughout its entire proposed length within three years from the date thereof.

II. That power and authority is hereby granted to and invested in the Board of Directors of this Company to cause to be executed, issued, sold and delivered, bonds thereof, under its corporate seal, payable forty years after date, with interest thereon at the rate of six per centum per annum, payable Semi-Annually, said interest to be evidenced by coupons to be attached to said bonds.

The amount of said bonds so to be executed, issued, sold, and delivered shall not exceed the sum of Twenty-Thousand Dollars for every mile of said road constructed and to be constructed.

The terms, denomination, date, place of payment, and other details in regard to bonds shall be prescribed by the Board of Directors.

III. That the power and authority is hereby granted to and invested in the Board of Directors of this Company to cause to be prepared and executed under its corporate seal and the signature of its President, and duly delivered and recorded such proper deed of trust or mortgage upon the property, works, privileges, franchises, roadways, sidings, depots, engines, cars, rolling stock, and all other real and personal property belonging or pertaining to this company, whether constructed or to be constructed, acquired or to be acquired, in possession or to come into possession thereof, as may be required to secure the prompt payment of said bonds, the coupons to be attached thereto, and all interest which which may accrue on said bonds.

Provided, That such conveyance shall not include debts due or to become due for subscriptions made or to be made by individuals, counties or corporations to the capital stock of said Company. The form, terms, conditions and details of said deed and the selection of the trustee therein to be determined by the Board of Directors.

16

IV. That the Board of Directors are especially authorized and empowered in making said deed of trust or mortgage to include therein, and thereby to assign, transfer and convey the lease of the property, works, rights, privileges and franchises which it is proposed to make to the Virginia Midland Railway Company, and which is authorized by the first of these resolutions together with the benefit of said interest in the rent reserved in said lease.

In making said Deed or Mortgage, such provisions shall be inserted as to dedicate the amount of such rent to the payment of the interest on said bonds, and should the Board of Directors deem best to the accumulation of a sinking fund for the purpose of redeeming the said bonds at or before maturity.

V. That the Board of Directors are requested to give effect to these resolutions as soon after their passage, as in their judgment is practicable.

On the adoption of these resolutions a stock vote was demanded, which resulted in their adoption by a unanimous vote—there being 4017½ votes cast in favor of the resolutions.

Judge T. J. Wilson now offered the following resolution, which was adopted :

Resolved, that the resolution passed at the general meeting of the stockholders at Winston, on the 25th and 26th of October, 1881, by which the bonds authorized to be issued by this Company, were limited to run for a period of 30 years, be and the same is hereby modified by striking out 30 and inserting in lieu thereof 40 years.

On motion by Dr. Wiley the meeting adjourned, subject to the call of the President.

J. W. ALSPAUGH,
Secretary.

STOCKHOLDER'S MEETING.

WINSTON, N. C., Nov. 15, 1882.

The Stockholders of the North Carolina Midland Railroad Company met at the office of the Company in Winston this day, and proceeded to organize by the election of H. W. Fries, Esq., chairman, and J. W. Alspaugh, Secretary.

On motion by Mr. Morehead a committee of three were appointed to verify proxies, the chair appointed J. W. Fries, W. A. Clement and P. D. Price. Pending the report of the committee on proxies, on motion by Dr. Wiley the meeting took a recess until 2 o'clock, to-day.

WEDNESDAY, Nov. 15, 2 o'clock. P. M.

The meeting met promptly at 2 o'clock, H. W. Fries in the chair. The committee on proxies now reported as follows, to wit :

Shares represented by person		140.
" " by proxy,		3,571½.
Total number of shares represented,		3,711½.

The proceedings of the several meetings of the Company, which had not heretofore been approved, were now read, and the same were approved.

Mr. Morehead now offered the following resolutions as supplemental to the resolutions adopted at the meeting of the stockholders of this Company, in August last, which, after consideration, were adopted by a stock vote —all the shareholders voting in the affirmative, the vote was declared unanimous. The resolutions were as follows :

The stockholders of the North Carolina Midland Railroad Company, in general meeting assembled, pursuant to notice, at Winston, North Carolina, on the 15th day of Nov., 1882, adopted the following resolutions :

I. That power and authority is hereby granted to and invested in the Board of Directors of this Company, to lease the rights, property and franchises thereof to the Virginia Midland Railway Company. for a term of ninty-nine years from the date thereof with the privilege on the part of the Virginia Midland Raiway Company of renewing forever; said lease shall include the real and personal property of said Company, its franchises corporate, rights and privileges and sidings, depots, shops, houses, bridges, and other works and property whether constructed, or to be constructed, and whether now in possession or hereafter to be acquired.

The consideration for said lease shall be the payment to this Company or to whomsoever it may designate by the said Virginia Midland Railway Company of an annual rental of one hundred and twenty-one thousand dollars per annum during the continuance of said lease with a further proviso that said Virginia Midland Railway Company shall assume in said lease the payment of the principal of the bonds for two millions of dollars which it is proposed this Company shall issue under the powers granted by the second of this series of resolutions. But provision may be made for the renewal of said bonds by this Company for such length of time as said Virginia Midland Railway Company may require and in case of such renewal at a lower rate of interest than six per centum per annum, there shall thereafter be a reduction of the annual rental above provided, by an amount equal to the amount of reduction in said interest, and when said Virginia Midland Railway Company shall pay off the principal of said debt, or any part thereof, there shall thereafter be a reduction in the amount of rental to be paid by it equal to the amount of annual interest on the principal so paid by it, with the limitation above set forth; the

date, terms, conditions and details of said lease shall be
such as may be determined and agreed upon by the
Board of Directors of this Company. In making said
lease authority is granted to the said Board of Directors
to covenant that the said road shall be completed
throughout its entire proposed length within three years
from the date thereof.

That power and authority is hereby granted to and invested in the Board of Directors of this Company to
cause to be executed, issued, sold, and delivered, bonds
thereof under its corporate seal payable forty years after
date with interest thereon at the rate of six per centum
per annum payable semi-annually, said interest to be
evidenced by coupons to be attached to said bonds. The
amount of said bonds to be executed, issued, sold and
delivered shall not exceed the sum of Twenty thousand
dollars for every mile of said road constructed and to be
constructed. Provision may be made for the renewal of
said bonds on such terms as the Virginia Midland Railway Company may designate, provided, the rate of interest thereon shall not exceed six per centum per
annum.

The terms, forms, denominations, date, place of payment and other details in regard to said bonds shall be
prescribed by the Board of Directors.

III. That power and authority is hereby granted to
and invested in the Board of Directors of this Company
to cause to be prepared and executed under its corporate
seal and the signature of its President and duly delivered
and recorded such proper deed of trust, or mortgage
upon the property, works, privileges, franchises, road-
way, sidings, depots, engines, cars, rolling stock and all
other real and personal property belonging or pertaining
to this Company, whether constructed or to be constructed, acquired or to be acquired, in possession or to come

into possession thereof as may be requisite to secure the prompt payment of the said bonds, the coupons to be attached thereto and all interest which may accrue on said bonds given in renewal or continuation of said bonds or any part thereof, and the interest thereon.

Provided, that such conveyance shall not include debts due or to become due for subscription made or to be made by individuals, counties or corporations to the capital stock of said Company. The form, terms, conditions and details of said deed and the selection of the trustee therein to be determined by the Board of Directors.

IV. That the Board of Directors are especially authorized and empowered in making said deed of trust or mortgage to include therein and thereby to assign, transfer and convey the lease of the property, works, rights, privileges and franchises which it is proposed to make to the Virginia Midland Railway Company and which is authorized by the first of these resolutions, together with the benefit of and interest in, the rent reserved in said lease.

In making said deed or mortgage such provisions shall be inserted as to dedicate the amount of such rent to the payment of the interest on said bonds, and should the Board of Directors deem best to the accumulation of a sinking fund for the purpose of redeeming the said bonds at or before maturity.

V. That the Board of Directors are requested to give effect to these resolutions as soon after their passage as in. their judgment is practical.

The chair announced that the election of officers was now in order.

On motion by Dr. Wiley the meeting proceeded to the election of a new board of Directors; a stock vote being demanded, the meeting proceeded to vote by ballot ;

Hon. T. J. Wilson being unanimously appointed to cast the votes of all the stockholders, when it appeared that the following gentlemen had received each 3711½ votes, being the entire number of shares represented in the meeting, and were therefore elected, to wit :

J. E. GILMER,
L. W. ANDERSON,
J. M. VAUGHN,
W. C. WILSON,
C. G. HOLLAND,
C. H. WILEY,
P. W. HAIRSTON,
A. M. BOOE,
A. LEAZAR,
J. WILCOX BROWN.

On motion by Mr. C. G. Holland this meeting now adjourned.

....

Chairman.

....

Secretary,

CONSOLIDATION OF THE N. C. M. R. R. CO. AND THE D. V. &. Y. R. N. G. R. R. CO.

Articles of agrement adopted by the Dan Valley and Yadkin River Railroad Company and the North Carolina Midland Railroad Company are as follows, to-wit :

This agreement made this the 22nd day of January, 1883, between the North Carolina Midland Railroad Company, a Company chartered and existing under the laws of the State of North Carolina of the first part, and the Dan Valley and Yadkin River Narrow Guage Railroad Company, a Company chartered and existing in the State of Virginia of the second part,

Witnesseth : That it is mutually covenanted and agreed,

I. That in accordance with the powers granted the first named of said contracting Company by the laws of the State of North Carolina and under and by virtue of the powers granted, the second party of said contracting Companies by its charter, the said two Companies, parties to this agreement, on and after the 1st day of March, 1883 shall be and hereby are of that date consolidated into one corporation, which shall be known under the name and style of " The North Carolina Midland Railroad Company," under which name it shall sue and be sued, contract and be contracted with and have all the power. and exercise all the rfghts, powers and franchises, granted to each of said Companies under their respective charters and by the general laws of the said two states of Virginia and North Carolina.

II. That terms and conditions of said consolidation of said two Companies shall be :

1. That the Capital stock of said consolidated and newly created Company shall be One Million Five Hundred Thousand Dollars ($1.500.000,) divided into shares the par value of which shall be One hundred dollars, and the holder of each share of stock in the component Companies respectively, shall be entitled to receive in lieu thereof one share of the capital stock of the consolidated Company, and after this Agreement has been fully consummated and has taken effect, the holder of such share in the component Companies, shall be, without further and more formal transfer, entitled to exercise all the rights and powers of a stockholder in said consolidated Company.

2. This joint agreement shall be carried into effect in the mode prescribed by the laws of the State of North Carolina, and by the charter of said Dan Valley and Yadkin River Narrow Gauge Railroad Company.

3. There shall be for said consolidated Railroad Com-

pany a President, a Vice President and twelve Directors, whose names and residences shall be, until their successors are elected; as follows :

President, Jno. S. Barbour, Alexandria, Va., Vice-President, J. Turner Morehead, Leaksville, N. C.

DIRECTORS :

A. S. BUFORD,	Richmond, Va.
A. Y. STOKES,	" "
A. LEAZAR,	Mooresville, N. C.
W. C. WILSON,	Mocksville' "
A. M. BOOE,	" "
C. H. WILEY,	Winston, "
JNO. W. FRIES,	Salem, "
L. W. ANDERSON,	Stokes Co., "
PETER W. HAIRSTON,	" "
J. M. VAUGHAN,	Madison, "
C. G. HOLLAND,	Danville, Va.
J. TURNER MOREHEAD,	Leaksville, N. C.

The President and Directors of said Company shall hereafter be annually elected by the stockholders of said Consolidated Company at their Annual Meeting to be held at such time and place as by the by-laws of said Company may be prescribed. The Vice-President shall be elected by the Board of Directors.

4. It shall be the duty of the Board of Directors of the said Consolidated Company within twelve months after the Consolidation proposed in this agreement has been fully consummated to call a general meeting of the stockholders of said Company, at which meeting a President and Board of Directors shall be elected to succeed those herein named, and all necessary by-laws, rules and regulations shall be adopted for the proper government of said Company.

Until said meeting is held, said Company shall be controlled in accordance with the general laws governing like Corporations.

III. The said Component Companies shall at once take such steps as may be necessary to consummate this Agreement whether prescribed by respective charters of said Companies, the Acts of Assembly of the States of Virginia and North Carolina, or the general laws governing Corporations of like powers and franchises.

This agreement is signed by Jno. S. Barbour, the President of the North Carolina Midland Railroad Company and the seal of said Company is hereto affixed, in obedience to a resolution of the Board of Directors of said Company adopted on the 15th day of November 1882, and it is signed by A. S. Buford the President of the Dan Valley and Yadkin River Narrow Gauge Railroad Company, and the seal of said Company is hereto affixed in obedience to a resolution of the Board of Directors of said Company, adopted on the 20th day of January, 1883.

And this agreement is attested by the signatures of said Presidents and the affixing of the said seals of said Companies respectively, to this paper.

THE N. C. MIDLAND R. R. CO.,
By J. S. Barbour, Pres.

A. S. BUFORD,
Pres. Dan Valley & Yadkin River Narrow Gauge R. R. Co.
(SEAL)

The undersigned Secretary of the meeting of the stock holders of the Dan Valley and Yadkin River Narrow Guage Railroad Company, held in the city of Richmond, Va., Saturday the 24th day of February, 1883, after due notice to said stockholders, hereby certifies that at said meeting the Agreement and Articles of Association and Consolidation of the Dan Valley and Yadkin River Narrow Guage Railroad Company, and the North Carolina

Midland Railroad Company were approved and adopted by fifty-five (55) votes, the same being all of the votes of all the stockholders of the Dan Valley and Yadkin River Narrow Guage Railroad Company.

In testimony whereof he has hereto subscribed his name and attached a scroll seal hereto—the said Company having no Corporate seal.   R. BROOKE,

Secy. of meeting of the stockholders of the Dan Valley and Yadkin River Narrow Gauge Railroad Company, held Feb. 24, 1883.

(SEAL)

———

The undersigned Secretary of the meeting of the stockholders of the North Carolina Midland Railroad Company, held in the city of Greensboro, N. C., on Wednesday the 14th day of March, 1883, after due notice to said stockholders, hereby certifies that at said meeting the Agreement and articles of association and consolidation of The Dan Valley and Yadkin River Narrow Gauge Railroad Company and The North Carolina Midland Railroad Company were approved and adopted by Three Thousand, Eight hundred and Sixty-two (3862) votes, the same being all of the votes of all the stockholders of the North Carolina Midland Railroad Company.

In testimony whereof he has hereunto subscribed his name and attached a seal hereto of said Company.

J. W. ALSPAUGH,

Secy. of meeting of stockholders of The North Carolina Midland Railroad Company, held March 14, 1883.

———

ANNUAL MEETING OF THE N. C. M. R. R. CO.

The stockholders of the Company met in the town of Winston pursuant to notice duly given by publication for more than thirty days.

On motion by J. T. Morehead, Esq., H. B. Howard was called to the chair, and J. W. Alspaugh was appointed Secretary.

On motion by J. W. Fries, Esq., a committee of three was appointed to verify proxies. The chairman appointed J. W. Fries, Dr. C. H. Wiley and J. B. McLelland.

Upon a call of the stocks, the committee reported present 3601 shares, which was more than a majority of the whole.

(See report of committee marked "A.")

Col. Buford moved that section 11 of the by-laws of the Company be amended by striking out the said section, and substituting therefor the following:

The administration of the affairs of this Company shall be vested in the President and twelve Directors who shall be elected annually by the stockholders, and they may appoint a Vice-President from their own body, and such other officers as from time to time they deem necessary for the proper dispatch of the business of the Company.

The meeting now proceeded to reorganize the Company by the election of a new board of officers.

J. T. Morehead was now elected President of the Company, and the following named gentlemen were chosen Directors under the amended section of the by-laws of the Company: A. S. Buford, W. P. Clyde, Baker, Scott, Huidikoper, McLeland, J. M. Vaughn, A. Leazar, J. W. Fries, W. C. Wilson, and C. H. Wiley.

On motion by Mr. Morehead, the Secretary and Treasurer was instructed to procure a stock book and certificates of stock for the company, and also a seal.

On motion by Mr. Buford, it was resolved that the Board of Directors be, and that they are hereby authorized to take such additional subscriptions to the stock of

the Company as they may find practicable and judiciary.
On motion by Mr. Leazar, the meeting adjourned.

J. W. ALSPAUGH.
Secretary.

STOCKHOLDER'S MEETING.

The Annual Meeting of the stockholders of the North Carolina Midland Railroad Company, met in the town of Winston, pursuant to notice duly published, on the 10th day of November, 1886.

Hon. J. T. Morehead, President of the Company in the chair.

Upon a call of the roll, the following gentlemen responded to their names: Messrs. J. W. Fries, A. Leazar. Maj. Clement, W. C. Wilson, F. M. Johnson, J. W. Alspaugh, H. W. Fries, and others.

On motion J. W. Alspaugh, Secretary and Treasurer, was requested to act as Secretary of the meeting.

On motion J. W. Fries, A. Leazar and Maj. Clement was appointed to verify proxies. Upon report of the committee it appeared that but 1064 shares were represented in the meeting—a number less than a majority of the whole, no business would be transacted, whereupon on motion by Mr. Leazar, it was resolved to adjourn this meeting to the 11th day of January, 1887, to meet in the city of Raleigh.

It was further ordered that the Secretary of the meeting give due and timely notice to all the absent members of the Company, of the meeting to be held in the city of Raleigh on the 11th day of January, 1887.

J. W. ALSPAUGH,
Secretary.

ADJOURNED MEETING OF THE STOCKHOLD-ERS HELD IN THE CITY OF RALEIGH, JANUARY 11th, 1887.

The meeting was called to order by the President, and on motion Rev. W. C. Wilson was elected Chairman, and Cabell Hairston, Secretary.

Committee to verify proxies, consisting of A. Leazar, J. W. Fries and W. A. Lash reported 4133 shares of stock represented in person and by proxy, as follows:

A. Leagar, 277½ shares; W. A. Lash, 2; J. W. Fries, 101; T. B. Baily, 5½; J. T. Morehead, 204; W. C. Wilson, 16; J. M. Vaughn, 119; W. B. Clements, 2; E. L. Gaither, 500; T. J. Wilson, 406; Col. A. B. Andrews, 2500.

After a statement made by Col. Andrews representing the stock of the Virginia Midland Railroad Company and at this request, Mr. A. Leazar offered a resolution which was adopted, that this meeting adjourn to meet in Greensboro on the 10th day of February, 1887.

W. C. WILSON,
Chairman.

CABELL HAIRSTON,
Secretary.

MEETING OF NORTH CAROLINA RESIDENT STOCKHOLDERS.

Pursuant to a call of the President, under what is known as the Leazar bill, the stockholders resident in North Carolina met in the city of Raleigh January 11th, 1887, an adjournment of the regular meeting as above.

The same committee on proxies reported 1633 shares of stock represented in person and by proxy.

J. W. Fries offered the following resolution:

Resolved, That...
be appointed agent and attorney of the individual and

corporate stockholders of the N. C. Midland R. R. Co., who may become subscribers to this resolution, to make application to the Attorney General of the State of N. C. for leave to bring an action in the name of the State, to annul the charter of the N. C. Midland R. R. Company.

.*Resolved further*, That all stockholders who may become parties to this action shall be jointly held and bound to the State of N. C. in a sum sufficient to indemnify the State against all costs and expenses of said action.

Resolved further, That this action to annul said charter shall be brought upon the grounds that,

1st, The Va. Midland R. R. Co. made a subscription for a majority of the capital stock of the N. C. Midland R. R. Co. on the condition that the subscription books should be then closed, and not reopened without its consent, and with the understanding that our road should be completed without unnecessary delay.

2nd. That after thus securing a majority of the stock in the N. C. Midland R. R. Co., the said Va. Midland R. R. Co. used the power thus acquired to defeat the purposes for which said N. C. Midland Co. was organized,—in that they did not push the building of said road themselves,— and in that, by holding this work in abeyance, they detered and prevented the individual and corporate stockholders along line of said road from uniting in other combinations, which would probably have secured railroad facilities to this section of the State.

3rd. That there has been no work whatever done on said railroad for more than two years consecutively, and that therefore the corporation should be annulled for non-user. user.

And on motion of T. J. Wilson the consideration of said resolution was postponed until the North Carolina resident stockholders shall meet again in Greensboro February 10th, 1887.

The following resolution, offered by Mr. Clements, was adopted:

Resolved, That the Secretary and Treasurer of the North Carolina Midland Railroad Company be requested to produce at the adjourned meeting of the North Carolina Midland Railroad at Greensboro, on the 10th of February, 1887, the stock or subscription books of said Company— the contract made by the Richmond and West Point Terminal Company signed by Genl. Logan, with John L. Barbour, to complete the North Carolina Midland Railroad,—the resolution of the Virginia Midland appropriating $50,000 to construction of the North Carolina Midland Railroad,—and all other books, together with an itimized statement of receipts and disbursements, with amount of outstanding indebtedness.

The Chairman was requested to call on Col. Andrews and notify him of the action of this meeeting. Motion was made and carried to adjourn to meet in Greensboro, February 10, 1887.

W. C. WILSON,
Chairman.

CABELL HAIRSTON,
Secretary.

ADJOURNED MEETING OF THE STOCKHOLDERS OF THE NORTH CAROLINA MIDLAND R. R. CO., HELD IN GREENSBORO, N. C., FEB. 10, 1887.

The meeting was called to order by the President, Col. J. T. Morehead, and on motion Maj. W. B. Clement was elected Chairman, and R. T. Stedman, Secretary. On motion by Col. J. T. Morehead, the following gentlemen were appointed a committee to verify proxies:

A. Leazar and J. W. Fries, and reported 4143½ shares represented.

A. Lezar offered the following resolutions, which were adopted:

WHEREAS, A. B. Andrews, third Vice-President of the R. & D. R. R. Co., and holding the proxy of the said Company's stock in the N. C. Midland R. R. Co., has presented the following resolutions, as adopted by the executive of the Board of Directors of the R. & D. R. R. Co., at their meeting held on the 8th day of February, 1887, in the city of New York, to wit:

Resolved, That it is the sense of the committee that the North Western N. C. R. R. should be extended from Winston to Wilkesboro, and that active operations be resumed on the N. C. Midland, and the portion of that road from Winston to Mocksville should be first constructed.

Resolved, That A. B. Andrews, third Vice-President, is hereby instructed to take the steps necessary to carry out this policy : and

WHEREAS, this is received as a proposition on the part of the R. & D. R. R. Co., made in good faith, and with the understanding that the work on the N. C. Midland R. R. from Winston to Mocksville is to be commenced within 90 days and prosecuted as named in said resolutions to completion.

Resolved, by the stockholders of the N. C. Midland R. R. Co., in general meeting assembled, 4143½ shares of the stock being represented, that the President and Directors are instructed to cooperate with A. B. Andrews and the R. & D. R. R. Co., in the immediate prosecution of the work from Winston to Mocksville as a part of the N. C. Midland R. R. and under the charter of said road.

On motion by Col. Morehead, it was resolved that when this meeting adjourns it adjourns to meet in Greensboro on the 11th day of May, 1887.

Col. A. B. Andrews offered the following resolution:

Resolved, That the election of officers of the N. C.

Midland R. R. Co., be postponed until the next meeting to be held on the 11th day of May, 1887.

On motion by Col. Andrews, J. W. Fries, J. T. Morehead and R. T. Stedman were appointed to ascertain the indebtedness, get up list of the stockholds, subscription books, &c., of the N. C. M. R. R. Co.

On motion the meeting adjourned.

W. B. CLEMENT,
Chairman.

R. T. STEDMAN,
Secretary.

MEETING OF RESIDENT N. C. STOCKHOLDERS.

Pursuant to a call of the President under what is known as the Leazar bill, the stockholders resident in N. C. met in Greensboro, February 10th, 1887.

On motion W. B. Clement was elected Chairman, and R. T. Stedman, Secretary. The committee on proxies reported 1643½ shares represented.

On motion by Mr. Fries the meeting adjourned to meet in Greensboro on the 11th day of May, 1887.

W. B. CLEMENT,
Chairman.

R. T. STEDMAN,
Secretary.

GREENSBORO, N. C. JUNE 29th, 1887.

Pursuant to adjournment of the 11th day of May, 1887, the stokcholders of the North Carolina Midland Railroad Company met in Greensboro, North Carolina, on Wednesday, the 29th day of June, 1887, at which time and place the following proceedings were had, to wit:

On motion, Hon. A. Leazar was called to the chair and D. Schenck, Jr., was requested to act as Secretary.

The minutes of the preceeding meeting were read and approved.

On motion of Col. A. B. Andrews, J. W. Fries and J. W. Clement were appointed a committee to verify proxies.

The committee on proxies reported 4093 shares of stock present, which was a majority of all the stock.

The report of the committee on indebtedness, list of stockholders, &c., was read by J. Turner Morehead, and was laid on the table on motion of Mr. Clement.

Mr. J. Turner Morehead offered the following resolution:

"*Resolved*, 1. That the Board of Directors of The North Carolina Midland Railroad Company is hereby authorised, empowered and directed, whenever they think proper, to issue the bonds of this Company to an amount not exceeding Fifteen Thousand Dollars ($15,-000.00) per mile of said road and to cause to be lawfully executed a Mortgage or trust conveying all the property, real and personal, and the franchises of the Company to secure said bonds, with such conditions and limitations as they may prescribe.

"And said Board of Directors is further authorised and empowered to issue certificates of stock of the corporation to an amount not exceeding Twenty-Five Thousand Dollars ($25,000) per mile of said road.

2. "That said Board of Directors be authorised and empowered to use the bonds and stock authorised to be issued, as above, for the purpose of constructing the said railroad from some point on the North Western North Carolina Railroad, near the town of Winston, to Mocksville, and to that end are authorised and empowered to make such contract with any Construction Company, or other party, as they may see proper, for the construction of said road, as aforesaid, and for that purpose may use the bonds and stock authorised to be issued, as above, in such manner as they may deem best, and, in general, said Board of Directors are authorised and empowered to do

any and all things in the premises as may be necessary to carry into effect the purposes and object of its resolutions.

3. "That the foregoing powers are not to be restricted by any former action of the stockholders and that any and all former actions and resolutions of the stockholders, inconsistent with the above resolutions, are hereby repealed."

To the foregoing resolution Mr. J. M. Galloway offered the following amendment:

"Provided—That Madison Township and the private subscribers therein be released from any further liability on their unpaid subscriptions."

The amendment was put and voted down.

The resolution was put and adopted.

The following resolution was offered by Mr. J. W. Fries:

"*Resolved*, That the President of this Company be authorised and directed to collate all the Charters, Acts of Incorporation and by-laws of this Company, and have the same printed for the use of the Company."

The resolution was put and adopted.

Mr. J. Turner Morehead offered the following resolution:

"*Resolved*, That the by-law enacted by the North Carolina Midland Railroad Company at its annual meeting and recorded on page 114 of the Record of Proceedings of the Company be stricken out and the following by-law be substituted for it, to wit:

"That the administration of the affairs of the Company shall be vested in a President and Board of Twelve Directors, and if the Board of Directors deem it best for the interest of the Company, a Vice-President, also.

"The Directors shall be elected by the stockholders at their annual meeting, by ballot.

The Board of Directors shall elect one of their number President of the Company, and may elect a Vice-President.

It shall require a majority of the Directors to be present to co 1stitute a quorum." Which was adopted.

The following Directors were elected:

A. LEAZAR.	ALFRED SULLY,
W. C. WILSON,	T. M. LOGAN,
J. W. FRIES,	GEO. F. SCOTT,
J. TURNER MOREHEAD,	J. B. PACE,
A. B. ANDREWS,	JAMES H. DOOLEY.
J. M. GALLOWAY,	D. SCHENCK.

There being no further business, on motion, the stockholders adjourned to meet at Greensboro, N. C., on Thursday, the 1st day of September, 1887.

A. LEAZAR,
Chairman.

D. SCHENCK, JR.,
Secretary.

ANNUAL MEETING.

WINTSON, NOV. 14, 1888.

•The stockholders of the N. C. Midland Railway met at the office of the First National Bank of Winston, on the 14th day of Nov. 1888. Upon a call of the names of the shareholders it appeared that the President of the Company was not present, and no business coming before the meeting, on motion of Geo. W. Hinshaw the meeting adjourned until the 24th inst., and the Secretary was authorized and instructed to notify the shareholders by postal of the adjourned meeting to take place on the 24th of November, 1888.

J. W. ALSPAUGH,
Secretary and Treasurer.

36

ANNUAL MEETING.

WINSTON, Nov. 24, 1888.

Stockholders meeting of the N. C. Midland Railway Co. held at Winston this day, being an adjourned meeting of the annual meeting of the 14th inst. On motion by Col. J. T. Morehead, Hon. T. J. Wilson was called to the chair, and J. W. Alspaugh was elected Secretary for the meeting.

On further motion by Col. Morehead, J. W. Fries and Geo. W. Hinshaw were appointed a committee to certify proxies. Upon a call of the list of stock the committee reported 3,376 shares represented out of 4,503, and that a majority of all the shares was represented in the meeting. Report filed. Col. Morehead made a verbal report and offered the following resolutions, which were adopted, to-wit:

Resolved, That article 11 of the By-Laws of the stockholders and the resolution passed at the meeting held in Greensboro, June 29th, 1887, be amended, so as to read: The administration of the affairs of the Company shall be vested in a board of 13 directors. The directors shall be elected annually by the stockholders by ballot and they shall elect one of their number President and one Vice-President.

WHEREAS, The interests of this Company and of its stockholders require that the steps necessary to build, construct, equip and put into operation its anthorized line of railroad from a point at or near the town of Winston, North Carolina, to a point at or near the town of Mocksville, North Carolina, and

WHEREAS, To facilitate such objects it is deemed to be judicious and proper that the stockholders should invest the directors with full power to act and proceed in all or any matters in the premises which might otherwise require action by the stockholders, therefore be it

Resolved, That the Board of Directors be, and hereby is, fully authorized and empowered to cause to be made all necessary surveys and locations of the line of railroad of this Company, extending from a point at or near the town of Winston, in the County of Forsyth, and State of North Carolina to a point at or near the town of Mocksville, in the County of Davie, in said State, and do all acts, and make all contracts, in the name and on behalf of the Company, which in its judgment may, from time to time, be requisite to locate and secure the right-of-way for said railroad, and to fully and properly build and construct the same, with necessary road-bed, rails, bridges, trestles, fixtures, depots, workshops, tenements, yards and other appurtenances, and to fully and effectively equip the same with locomotives, cars, and other rolling stock, and appurtenances thereto, and to provide the ways and means necessary thereto and therefor, and that the said Board of Directors be, and hereby is, fully authorized and empowered in its discretion to contract in the name and on behalf of this Company with any persons, parties or corporations, in order to carry out and accomplish the objects, ends and purposes aforesaid.

BY-LAW.

Resolved, That the following be, and hereby is, adopted as a by-law of this Company to be in force from and after this date, viz:

Art. XIX—The Board of Directors may appoint an executive committee to consist of two members, exclusive of the President, who shall be ex-officio a member and Chairman thereof, which committee, acting by a majority of its members, shall have and exercise all the powers of the Board of Directors in the management of the business and affairs of the Company, subject to such special directions in regard thereto as the Board of Directors may give.

Said committee shall meet at such times and places as it may determine, and shall keep a record of all its proceedings, and report the same to the Board as may by it be requested.

The meeting now proceeded to the election of a new Board of Directors, which resulted as follows, upon a stock vote:

J. H. T. Woman, of N. Y.; C. S. Brice, of N. Y.; W. G. Oakman, of N. Y; J. A. Rutherford; J. C. Mauen; J. Turner Morehead, Leaksville; J. W. Fries, Salem; A. Leazar, Moorsville; G. W. Hinshaw, Winston; F. M. Johnson, Farmington; W. C. Wilson, Mocksville, A. B. Andrews, Raleigh.

Blank to be supplied by the Board of Directors.

On motion the meeting adjourned.

J. W. ALSPAUGH,
Secretary.

DIRECTORS MEETING.

RALEIGH, N. C. JANUARY, 16, 1889.

Subject to the call of the President the Directors of the North Carolina Midland R. R. Co. met in the office of Col. A. B. Andrews; the following gentlemen were present:

J. Turner Morehead, A. Leazar, G. W. Hinshaw, J. W. Fries, F. M. Johnson and A. B. Andrews.

On motion of Col. Andrews Hon. T. B. Baily was elected to fill the place in the Board of Directors left open by the stockholders at their meeting November 24th, 1888.

Maj. J. Turner Morehead resigned the Presidency and on motion Col. A. B. Andrews was elected to fill the vacancy. On motion Maj. J. Turner Morehead was elected Vice-President.

Mr. R. Brooke was elected Secretary in the place of

Col. J. W. Alspaugh, and H. W. Miller Assistant Secretary.

Mr. John W. Hall elected Treasurer.

There being no other business before the Directors they adjourned to meet subject to call of President.

H. W. MILLER,
Assistant Secretary.

ANNUAL MEETING.

WINSTON, N. C., NOV. 13, 1889.

The stockholders of the N. C. Midland R. R. Co. met as per by-laws; there not being sufficient shares represented the meeting was adjourned to meet the 14th day of March, 1890.

H. W. MILLER,
Assistant Secretary.

CHAPTER 37.—AN ACT

To Incorporate the Dan Valley and Yadkin
River Narrow-Guage Railroad Company.

Approved January 27, 1879.

1. Be it enacted by the general assembly of Virginia,
That it shall be lawful to open books of subscription at
the town of Danville, Virginia, and such other places as
the commissioners hereinafter named shall designate, under the direction of C. G. Holland, E. B. Withers, F. M.
Hamlin, Daniel Coleman, F. B. Gravely, Charles W.
Venable, —— Smith, J. T. Morehead, Peter W. Hairston,
J. G. Brodnax, Joseph H. Scales, S. G. Sheffield, W. T.
Sutherlin, J. M. Neal, J. E. Schoolfield, W. P. Robinson,
J. R. Wilson, R. R. Robinson, John F. Rison, R. L. Hick-
son, H. W. Cole, T. J. Talbott, H. D. Guerrant, or any
five of them, and such other persons as they may appoint,
for the purpose of receiving subsrciptions to the capital
stock of the Dan Valley and Yadkin River Narrow-Gauge
Railroad Company to an amount not exceeding five hundred thousand dollars, in shares of one hundred dollars
each, to constitute a joint capital stock for the construction of a railroad from the town of Danville, Virginia, up
or near the Dan River Valley in the direction of Leaksville, North Carolina, to the North Carolina line.

2. Be it further enacted, That whenever fifty thousand
dollars shall have been subscribed to the capital stock of said
road, whether by individuals, corporations, cities, or towns,
the subscribers, their executors, administrators, and assigns,
shall be and they are hereby declared and constituted a body
politic and corporate, under the name and style of The
Dan Valley and Yadkin River Narrow-Guage Railroad
Company, and as such shall be entitled to all the privileges conferred and subject to all the restrictions imposed
by the Code of Virginia, edition of eighteen hundred and

seventy-three, and acts amendatory thereof, so far as the same are applicable, and not inconsistent with this act.

. 3. It shall be lawful to secure subscription to the capital stock of said company in money, labor, land, or materials, such as timber, stone, lumber, or supplies of any kind usually required in the construction of a railroad; and it shall also be lawful to receive the bonds of any city, town, county, or township at par in payment of subscriptions; and said company may also acquire land by gift or purchase, and shall have power to hold and sell the same for the construction or repair of their road, for depots, or other necessary purposes.

4. The said company shall have power to build branch or lateral roads, not exceeding twenty-five miles in length, to connect with any mines, iron works, or other manufactories.

5. Subscriptions to the capital stock of this company may be made by individuals, the town of Danville, and by any city, town, county or township, and by any railroad company, or any mining or manufacturing company.

6. It shall be lawful for said railroad company to borrow money for the construction, maintenance, and repair of its road or any branch thereof; and also to issue bonds, and secure the same by mortgaging its property and franchises, or otherwise.

7. It shall be lawful for said company to lease out its road, property, rights and franchises to individuals, or to any other company or corporation; also to lease the road, property, rights and franchises of any other company connecting with said company's road; also to consolidate its stock and property with that of any other company connecting with it, whether chartered by this or any other state; also to make any contract or agreement by which the road-bed and rolling stock of said company, or any

part thereof, may be constructed and used, in whole or in part, by the Danville and New River narrow-gauge railroad company, or any other company whose line of railroad shall connect with said company's road.

8. Whenever the company and the land owners cannot agree for the use of land along the line of the company's road, commissioners shall be appointed, as provided for by law, to ascertain the value of the same. Said commissioners so appointed shall, on ascertaining the damages, take into consideration the advantages and benefits to accrue to such land owner by the construction of said road through his or her land.

9. It shall be lawful, with the consent of North Carolina, for the company organized under this charter to extend its road into the state of North Carolina at or near Leaksville.

10. This act shall be in force from its passage.

CHAPTER 255.—AN ACT

To Amend the Charter of the Dan Valley and Yadkin River Railroad Company.

Approved March 3, 1879.

Be it further enacted, That by and with the consent of the State of North Carolina, the Dan Valley and Yadkin river narrow-gauge railroad company shall have the right to extend its road, with all the rights, privileges and franchises given and granted under and by this charter into the State of North Carolina, through the counties of Rockingham, Forsythe, Stokes, Yadkin and Wilkes, or either of them, and such other counties as may be necessary to reach the most desirable connection with any other railroad, and the crossing of the mountains to the Tennessee line.

DANVILLE, VA., Aug. 31st, 1880.

At a meeting of the stockholders of the Dan Valley and Yadkin River Narrow Gauge Railroad, held at the office of E. B. Withers, Danville, Va., at 10 o'clock, a. m., this day in accordance with the notice heretofore published in the Danville Post, the following resolutions were adopted:

WHEREAS, The commissioners have reported that the requisite amount of stock has been subscribed to organize the company and the amount of two per centum paid thereon as the law directs. Therefore, be it

RESOLVED, That we proceed to organize the Company.

On motion of W. T. Sutherlin, Col. E. B. Withers was elected chairman and F. M. Hamlin, Secretary.

On motion it was resolved that this meeting adjourn to meet on Wednesday, September 15th, at the office of E. B. Withers, Danville, Va,, at 11 o'clock, a. m.

E. B. WITHERS,
Chairman.

F. M. HAMLIN,
Secretary.

DANVILLE, VA., Sept. 15th, 1880.

At an adjourned meeting of the stockholders of the Dan Valley and Yadkin River Narrow-Guage Railroad held at the office of E. B. Withers, pursuant to adjournment,

On motion of Thos. J. Talbott the meeting adjourned to meet at 10 o'clock, September 16th, at the office of E. B. Withers.

E. B. WITHERS,
Chairman.

F. M. HAMLIN,
Secretary.

DANVILLE, VA., Sept. 16th, 1880.

At a meeting of the stockholders of the Dan Valley and Yadkin River Narrow Gauge Railroad held at the office of E. B. Withers, this day at 10 o'clock, a. m., .pursuant to adjournment,

The Chairman on motion appointed a Committee of Col. A. S. Buford, T. J. Talbott and W. T. Sutherlin, to ascertain and report if a majority of the stock subscribed was represented. The committee reported fifty-five shares of stock represented in person and proxy, being a majority of the stock subscribed.

On motion of Major W. T. Sutherlin it was moved and seconded that the company be organized by the election of a President, and board of six directors: Col. A. S. Buford was nominated and unanimously elected President of the company. The names of the following gentlemen suggested by Major W. T. Sutherlin were elected the the board of directors, viz:

E. B. WITHERS,   THOS. J. TALBOTT,
A. Y. STOKES,   T. M. LOGAN,
JOHN P. BRANCH,   F. M. HAMLIN.

1. On motion it was resolved that the President and board of directors be authorized to prepare and adopt for the government of the Company such by-laws and regulations as they shall deem necessary, and to appoint such additional officers and agents of the company, as they shall from time to time find necessary for the proper organization and conduct of the company's affairs, and work; and shall prescribe the compensation to be paid to all the officers and agents of the Company.

2. *Resolved*, That the board of directors shall be authorized in their discretion to appoint, out of their own body, a Vice-President, with such authority and duties as in their judgement may be necessary and useful.

3. *Resolved*, That the board be authorized and requested to provide as soon as practicable for such surveys of
the proposed line of road in their State and to take such
steps towards its extension as contemplated in the State
of North Carolina as in their judgement will best forward
the early and successful progress of the enterprize.

4. *Resolved*, That the President and Board of Directors
be and they are hereby authorized, to call for payment
of subscription as may be requisite, and to take such
steps for obtaining additional subscription as they think
proper and to provide as they may find practicable the
necessary means of prosecuting the company's work with
energy and dispatch.

5. *Resolved*, That the regular annual meeting of the
stockholders of this company be held on the 2nd Wednesday of November of each year in the city of Danville,
Va., or at such other place as may be designated by the
President and board of Directors. Adopted.

6. On motion of Col. A. S. Buford the meeting adjourned.

E. B. WITHERS,

Chairman.

F. M. HAMLIN,

Secretary.

RICHMOND, VA., Feb. 24th, 1883.

A general meeting of the stockholders of the Dan
Valley and Yadkin River Narrow-Gauge Railroad Company was held at the office of the Richmond and Danville Railroad Company, at 12 o'clock, M., this day,
pursuant to the following notice duly published according to law, for thirty days in the Richmond *Dispatch*,
viz :

" NOTICE.—A General Meeting of the Stockholders

of the Dan Valley and Yadkin River Narrow-Guage
Railroad Company will be held at the office of the
Richmond and Danville Railroad Company, in the
City of Richmond, Va., on the 24th day of Feb. 1883,
at 12 o'clock, M.

By order of the Board of Directors.

A. S. BUFORD,
President."

The meeting was called to order by A. S. Buford,
President of the Company; And, on his motion, A. Y.
Stokes, Esq,, was called to the chair, and R. Brooke was
requested to act as Secretary of the meeting.

The Chairman requested the Secretary to ascertain
and report whether or not a quorum of the Stockholders
was present, and the Secretary reported that all of the
stock of the Company, being fifty-five (55) shares, was
represented in the meeting, either by stockholders in
person, or by their proxies, duly appointed.

The President stated, that the meeting had been called
for the purpose of taking such action as the stockholders
might deem proper, on an agreement between this Company and the North Carolina Midland Railroad Company, providing for a consolidation of the two Companies,
which said Agreement had been approved by the North
Carolina Midland Railroad Company, through its Board
of Directors and Stockholders, and by the Board of Directors of this Company on the 20th day of January, 1883,
subject to the ratification of the stockholders, and which
was in the following words and form, to-wit:

This Agreement made this 22nd day of January, 1883,
between the North Carolina Midland Railroad Company,
a Company chartered and existing under the laws of the
State of North Carolina, of the first part, and the Dan
Valley and Yadkin River Narrow-Guage Railroad Com-

pany, a Company chartered and existing under the laws
of the State of Virginia, of the second part, Witnesseth:

That it is mutually Covenanted and agreed:

1. That, in accordance with powers granted the first
named of said contracting Companies by the laws of the
State of North Carolina, and under and by virtue of
the powers granted the second of said contracting
Companies by its charter, the said two Companies,
parties to this Agreement, on and after the 1st day of
March, 1883, shall be, and hereby are of that date consolidated into one corporation, which shall be known
under the name and style of " *The North Carolina Midland Railroad Company*," under which name it shall sue
and be sued, contract and be contracted with, and pos-
sess and exercise all the rights, powers and franchises
granted to each of said Companies under their respective
charters and by the general laws of the said two States of
Virginia and North Carolina.

2. The terms and conditions of said Consolidation of
said two Companies shall be:

1. That the capital stock of said consolidated and newly created Company shall be One Million five hundred
thousand dollars ($1,500,000,) divided into shares, the
par value of which shall be One hundred dollars, and the
holder of each share of stock in the Component Companies respectively shall be entitled to receive in lieu thereof one share of the capital stock of the consolidated Company, and after this Agreement has been fully consummated and has taken effect the holder of such share in
the component companies, shall be, without further and
more formal transfer, entitled to exercise all the rights
and powers of a stockholder in said consolidated Company.

2. This joint agreement shall be carried into effect in

the mode prescribed by the laws of the State of North
Carolina, and by the charter of said Dan Valley and Yadkin River Narrow-Gauge Railroad Company.

3. There shall be for said Consolidated Railroad Company, a President, a Vice President and twelve Directors,
whose names and residences shall be, until their successors are elected, as follows:

President, John S. Barbour, Alexandria, Va., Vice-
President, J. Turner Morehead, Leaksville, N. C.

DIRECTORS:

A. S. BUFORD,	Richmond, Va.
A. Y. STOKES,	" "
A. LEAZAR,	Mooresville, N. C.
W. C. WILSON,	Mocksville, "
A. M. BOOE,	" "
C. H. WILEY,	Winston, N. C.
JOHN W. FRIES,	Salem, "
L. W. ANDERSON,	Stokes Co., "
PETER W. HAIRSTON,	" " "
J. M. VAUCHAN,	Madison, "
C. G. HOLLAND,	Danville, Va.
J. TURNER MOREHEAD,	Leaksville, N. C.

The President and Directors of said Company shall
hereafter be annually elected by the stockholders of said
consolidated Company at their Annual Meeting to be
held at such time and place as by the By-Laws of said
Company may be prescribed. The Vice President, shall
be elected by the Board of Directors.

4. It shall be the duty of the Board of Directors of the
consolidated Company, within twelve months after the
consolidation proposed in this Argeement has been fully
consummated, to call a general meeting of the stockholders of said Company at which meeting a President
and Board of Directors shall be elected to succeed those

herein named, and all necessary By-Laws, rules and regulations shall be adopted for the proper government of said Company.

Until said meeting is held, said Company shall be controlled in accordance with the general laws governing like corporations.

3. The said component Companies shall at once take such steps as may be necessary to consummate this Agreement, whether prescribed by the respective charters of said Companies, the Acts of Assembly of the States of. Virginia and North Carolina, or the general laws governing corporations of like powers and franchises·

This Agreement is signed by John S. Barbour, the President of the North Carolina Midland Railroad Company, and the seal of said Company is hereto affixed, in obedience to a resolution of the Board of Directors of said Company adopted on the 15th day of November, 1882, and it is signed by A. S. Buford, the President of the Dan Valley and Yadkin River Narrow-Gauge Railroad Company, and the seal of said Company is hereto affixed, in obedience to a resolution of the Board of Directors of said Company, adopted on the 20th day of January, 1883.

And this Agreement is attested by the signatures of said Presidents and the affixing of the said seals of said Companies respectively to this paper.

A. S. BUFORD,

President of the Dan Valley and Yadkin River Narrow-Guage
 [SEAL.]   *Railroad Company.*

And, after full consideration of the said Agreement, on motion, the following resolution was unanimously adopted, viz:

Resolved, That the Agreement of consolidation between this Company and the North Carolina Midland ·

Railroad Company, a copy of which has been submitted to this meeting, which the President was authorized to execute by the Board of Directors of this Company subject, however, to the approval and satisfaction of the stockholders in general meeting assembled, and which has already been approved and authorized by the stockholders of the North Carolina Midland Railroad Company, be and the same is hereby ratified and confirmed.

There being no further business before the meeting, on motion, the meeting adjourned.

A. Y. STOKES,
Chairman.

R. BROOKE,
Secretary.

CHAPTER 23.—AN ACT

TO ALLOW LEAKSVILLE TOWNSHIP, IN ROCKINGHAM COUNTY, TO SUBSCIBE TO THE CAPITAL STOCK OF A RAILROAD.

The General Assembly of North Carolina do enact:

SECTION 1. That Leaksville township, in Rockingham county, and any other township in said county, shall have power and authority to subscribe for and take any number of shares of the capital stock of the "Dan Valley and Yadkin River Railroad Company," or of any other railroad company, which has been or may hereafter be chartered to run through said county, that a majority of the legal voters of any such township may elect to take therein: *Provided*, that the valuation of the shares so subscribed for shall not exceed (5) five per cent. of taxable property of such township.

SEC. 2. That upon the written application of thirty residents and tax-payers of any such township, specifying the amount which it is desired that the said township

shall subscribe for in the capital stock aforesaid, subject
to the aforesaid limitations, it shall be the duty of the
county commissioners to appoint a day on which an election shall be held in such township in the manner prescribed by law for holding other elections, at which said
election the legally qualified voters of such township shall
be entitled to vote for or against such subscription, the
legally qualified voters favoring subscription to vote ballots written or printed " subscription," and those opposing
subscription to vote ballots writen or printed "no subscription." The election herein provided for shall be held
after thirty (30) days notice at the court house door and
in three other public places in said township, at the usual
voting places of such township, by persons appointed by
the county commissioners aforesaid in the same manner
that persons are appointed for holding other elections in
such township, and the returns thereof shall be made to
the county commissioners aforesaid as in other elections
prescribed by law, and who shall examine the same and
declare the result, and the commissioners shall meet for
this purpose at the court house on the day after the election or at their next regular meeting.

SEC. 3. And the result of said election as declared by
said commissioners shall be certified to by said county
commissioners under their hands and seal, and shall be
filed with the register of deeds of said county, and shall
be taken as evidence of the same in any of the courts of
this State.

SEC. 4. If the result of such election shall show that a
majority of the qualified voters of such township favor
taking the amount of stock voted for in such election, then
the said county commissioners shall appoint a board of
trustees, to be composed of five (5) resident tax-payers of
any such township, who shall issue the bonds of said township to an amount not exceeding the amount voted for in

said election, in sums of one hundred dollars and multiples thereof to one thousand dollars, running thirty years from date and bearing interest at eight per centum, payable semi-annually, evidenced by coupons on said bonds, and said board of trustees may deliver said bonds to said railroad company, or may sell the bonds and deliver the proceeds to said company, the said company, in either case issuing to the said trustees for the use and benefit of said township, stock in said company to the amount of the subscription so voted as aforesaid or any part thereof.

SEC. 5. That to provide for the interest on said bonds and their redemption at maturity the board of county commissioners aforesaid shall in addition to other taxes, each year compute and levy on all property and polls of any such township, preserving the constitutional equation, a sufficient tax to pay said interest, and after ten years a second additional tax sufficient to provide each year the sum of one thousand dollars for a sinking fund, which amount shall be annually paid to the county treasurer or other officer authorized by law to perform his duties, and by him invested in said bonds and the amount of tax collected for interest shall be paid to the county treasurer or other officer as aforesaid, and used by him in the prompt and regular payment of the coupons on said bonds.

SEC. 6. The county treasurer or other officer acting as such, shall, before buying the bonds with the sinking fund aforesaid, advertise for the purchase of said bonds, and in case none are offered the township, through the treasurer or other officer aforesaid, shall have power to call in the bonds aforesaid in whole or in part for payment, and in case the treasurer or other officer aforesaid shall buy the said bonds for less than par shall be entitled to receive only what he actually paid for the same.

SEC. 7. The capital stock held by any such township

voting as aforesaid, in any such railroad aforesaid, shall be pledged for the redemption of said bonds at maturity, and all dividends declared upon such stock shall be faithfully applied to the payment of the coupons on such bonds and to the purchase of the same, and be paid by said rail road company directly to the officer acting as county treasurer aforesaid, and by him used for the purpose aforesaid.

SEC. 8. In advertising the day of election aforesaid, the board of commissioners shall specify in such notice not only the amount of the subscription to be voted on, but also in what company it is proposed to subscribe for the capital stock aforesaid.

SEC. 9, This act shall take effect from its ratification.

Read three times in the general assembly and ratified the 8th day of February, A. D. 1879.

CHAPTER 60.—AN ACT

FOR THE BENEFIT OF THE WINSTON, SALEM AND MOORESVILLE RAILROAD COMPANY.

The General Assembly of North Carolina do enact:

SECTION 1. The board of directors of the penitentiary shall, on application of the chairman of the board of directors of said railroad company, or the president of said road, or an authorized agent, to employ on said road under the direction of the authorities of said road, and under such guards as may be necessary, as many convicts as in the opinion of the chairman of the board of directors of said railroad company, or the president of said road, as may be required, not to exceed one hundred and fifty, said convicts to be governed by and according to prison rules and regulations and under the supervision and control of a superintendent appointed by and subject to the penitentiary board: *Provided, however*, that the authorities of the road upon which convicts may work shall pay the hire of said superintendent, and gaurd, feed and clothe and properly care for said convicts while employed upon the said road: *Provided*, that there shall be an estimate of the net value of all the work done by the convicts' labor furnished by the State on the said railroad of the said company, and that the net value of such labor shall be a first mortgage in favor of the State upon the property and franchise of the said company. The value of the labor of said convicts shall be ascertained by two commissioners, one to be appointed by the governor and one to be selected by the said railroad company.

SEC. 2. The convicts obtained under this act shall be worked upon said road until the completion of the grading of said road.

SEC. 3. That the said chairman of the said board of directors of said railroad company, or the president of said road, shall before receiving the same from the directors of the penitentiary aforesaid, execute a receipt stating the names of said convicts, the county where and the offense of which he was convicted, and the term of his sentence; and at the expiration of the sentence, or the completion of the road, the president of the said road shall deliver the said convicts to the authorities of the penitentiary as the case may be.

SEC. 4. Nothing in this act contained shall be construed to interfere with or take away any of the convicts assigned to any railroad in which the State has an interest.

SEC. 5. That this act shall be in force from and after its ratification.

Ratified the 22nd day of February, A. D. 1879.

CHAPTER 113.—AN ACT

To aid in the Construction of the Winston, Salem and Mooresville Railroad.

The General Assembly of North Carolina do enact:

Section 1 That for the purpose of aiding in the construction of the Winston, Salem and Mooresville Railroad, the following named counties, towns, and townships are authorized in the manner hereinafter provided to subscribe not exceeding the sums herein named to the capital stock of said railroad company, to-wit: Davie county not exceeding the sum of fifty thousand dollars; the town of Mocksville not exceeding the sum of ten thousand dollars ; the township of Mocksville not exceeding the sum of fifteen thousand dollars; the township of Farmington not exceeding the sum of fifteen thousand dollars; the township of Jerusalem not exceeding the sum of ten thousand dollars; Coddle Creek township, in Iredell county, not exceeding the sum of twenty thousand dollars; the townships of Mount Ulla and Scotch Irish, in Rowan county, not exceeding the sums of fifteen thousand dollars each; the townships of Forbush and Little Yadkin, in Yadkin county, not exceeding the sums of ten thousand dollars each, and the township of Lewisville, in Forsythe county, not exceeding the sum of ten thousand dollars.

Sec. 2. That no such county, town or township shall be authorized to make any such subscription unless by a vote of a majority of all the voters entitled to vote therein, as hereinafter provided.

Sec. 3. The several townships herein mentioned are created municipal corporations and bodies politic and corporate, and by their respective township names may sue and be sued, implead and be impleaded, may have and use a corporate seal, and do all such other acts usually pertaining to municipal corporations, and the justices of the peace for each of said township shall be the board of trustees of each township respectively.

SEC. 4. Upon the written request of one-fifth of all the qualified voters in Davie county, the board of commissioners of said county are authorized and commanded to cause an election to be held at the several precincts in said county for the purpose of submitting to the qualified voters thereof the question of subscribing to the capital stock of said railroad company a sum not exceeding fifty thousand dollars, the exact amount of said subscription to be determined by the wishes of those signing the written request or petition above mentioned.

SEC. 5. If a majority of all the qualified voters of Davie county at said election shall vote for "subscription," then the said commissioners shall subscribe the sum so voted to the capital stock of said company, and shall pay said subscription to said company in such manner as said commissioners shall believe to be best to promote and advance the construction and completion of said railroad.

SEC. 6. In payment of said subscription the commissioners of Davie county shall issue bonds in the name of said county, in sums of one hundred dollars and in multiples thereof to one thousand dollars, running not exceeding twenty years from date, and bearing interest at a rate not exceeding seven per cent., payable semi-annually, evidenced by coupons on said bonds.

SEC. 7. To provide for the interest on said bonds and their redemption at maturity, the board of commissioners of said county shall, in addition to the other taxes in each year, compute and levy upon all the property in said county a sufficient tax to pay said interest and provide a sinking fund equal to five per centum of the original principal of said bonds, which amount shall be annually paid over to the county treasurer and invested by him in said bonds at par; and the amount of taxes collected for interest shall be paid to said county treasurer and used by him in the prompt and regular payment of the coupons upon said bonds.

SEC. 8. The capital stock held by said county in said railroad company shall be pledged for the redemption of said bonds at maturity, and all dividends declared upon each stock shall be faithfully applied to the payment of the coupons on said bonds, and shall be paid by said company directly to said county treasurer, and by him used for such purposes and no other.

SEC. 9. Said coupons shall be receivable in payment of all taxes due to the county of Davie.

SEC. 10. Upon the written request or petition of one-fifth of all the qualified voters of the town of Mocksville, the municipal authorities of said town are authorized and directed to cause an election to be held in said town for the purpose of submitting to the qualified voters thereof the question of subscribing to the capital stock of said railroad company a sum not exceeding ten thousand dollars, the exact amount to be determined by the wishes of those signing the written request or petition above mentioned.

SEC. 11. If a majority of all the qualified voters of said town at said election shall vote for "subscription," then the municipal authorities of said town shall subscribe the sum so voted to the capital stock of said company, and shall pay said subscription to said company in such manner as said municipal authorities shall believe to be best to promote and advance the construction and completion of said railroad.

SEC. 12. In payment of said subscription the said town shall issue bonds and levy taxes to provide for the payment of the coupons and a sinking fund in the same way as hereinbefore authorized to be done by Davie county.

SEC. 13. Upon the written request of one-fifth of all the qualified voters of each of the townships of Mocksville, Farmington and Jerusalem, the commissioners of Davie county are authorized and directed to cause an election to be held in said townships for the purpose of submitting to the qualified voters of each township separately the question of subscribing to the capital stock of said railroad company a sum not exceeding the amounts hereinbefore authorized to be so subscribed by each township respectively, the exact amount of each township subscription to be determined by the wishes of those signing the written request as aforesaid. But this section shall not be in force if the county of Davie shall make the subscription hereinbefore authorized.

SEC. 14. If a majority of all the qualified voters of either of said townships shall at said election vote for " subscription," then the said county commissioners on behalf of such township shall subscribe the sum so voted to the capital stock of said company, and shall pay said subscription to said company in such manner as the said commissioners on consultation with the justices of the peace of said township shall believe to be best to promote and advance the construction and completion of said railroad.

. SEC. 15. In payment of said subscription the said commissioners shall issue bonds and levy taxes on all the property of said township to provide for the payment of the coupons and a sinking fund in the same way as hereinbefore authorized to be done by said county of Davie.

SEC. 16. Upon the written request of one-fifth of all the qualified voters of each of the townships of Forbush and Little Yadkin the commissioners of Yadkin county are authorized and directed to cause an election to be held

in said townships for the purpose of submitting to the
qualified voters of each township separately the question
of subscribing to the capital stock of said company a sum
not exceeding the amount hereinbefore authorized to be
so subscribed by each township, the exact amount of
each township subscription to be determined by the
wishes of those signing the said written request.

SEC. 17. If a majority of all the qualified voters of
either of said townships shall at said election vote for
" subscription," then the said county commissioners on
behalf of such township shall subscribe the sum so
voted to the capital stock of said company, and shall pay
said subscription to said company in such manner as the
said commissioners on consultation with the justices of
the peace of said township shall believe to be best to promote and advance the construction and completion of
said railroad.

SEC. 18. In payment of said subscription the said commissioners shall issue bonds and levy taxes on all the
property of said township to provide for the payment
of the coupons and a sinking fund in the same way as
hereinbefore authorized to be done by the county of
Davie.

SEC. 19. Upon the written request of all [one-fifth] the
qualified voters of Lewisville township the commissioners of
Forsythe county are authorized and directed to cause an
election to be held in said township for the purpose of
submitting to the qualified voters thereof the question
of subscribing to the capital stock of said company a sum
not exceeding ten thousand dollars, the exact amount to
be determined by the wishes of those signing the said
written request.

SEC. 20. If a majority of all the qualified voters of said
township shall vote for " subscription," then the commissioners of Forsythe county on behalf of said township

shall subscribe the sum so voted to the capital stock of said company in such manner as said commissioners on consultation with the justices of the peace of said township shall believe to be best to promote and advance the construction and completion of said railroad.

Sec. 21. In payment of said subscription the said commissioners shall issue bonds and levy taxes on all the property of said township to provide for the payment of the coupons and a sinking fund in the same way as hereinbefore authorized for Davie county.

Sec. 22. Upon the written request of one-fifth of all the qualified voters of Mount Ulla and Scotch Irish townships the commissioners of Rowan county are authorized and directed to cause an election to be held in said townships for the purpose of submitting to the qualified voters of each township separately the question of subscribing to the capital stock of said company a sum not exceeding the amounts hereinbefore authorized to be so subscribed by each township, the exact amount of each township subscription to be determined by the wishes of those signing the said written request.

Sec. 23. If a majority of all the qualified voters of either of said townships shall at said election vote for "subscription," then the county commissioners of Rowan county on behalf of such township shall subscribe the sum so voted to the capital stock of said company in such manner as the said commissioners on consultation with the justices of the peace of said township shall believe to be best to promote and advance the construction and completion of said railroad.

Sec. 24. In payment of said subscription the said commissioners shall issue bonds and levy taxes on all the property in said township to provide for the payment of the coupons and a sinking fund in the same way as hereinbefore authorized to be done by the county of Davie.

SEC. 25. Upon the written request of one-fifth of all the voters of Coddle Creek township, the board of commissioners of Iredell county are authorized and directed to cause an election to be held in said township for the purpose of submitting to the qualified voters thereof the question of subscribing to the capital stock of said railroad company in a sum not exceeding twenty thousand dollars, the exact amount to be determined by the wishes of those signing the said request.

SEC. 26. If a majority of all the qualified voters of said township at said election shall vote for "subscription," then the said commissioners shall subscribe on behalf of said township the sum so voted to the capital stock of said company, in such manner as said commissioners on consultation with the justices of the peace of said township shall believe to be best to promote and advance the construction and completion of said railroad.

SEC. 27. In payment of said subscription the said commissioners shall issue bonds and levy taxes upon all the property in said township to provide for the payment of the coupons and a sinking fund, in the same way as hereinbefore authorized to be done by the county of Davie.

SEC. 28. At every election herein authorized, those in favor of subscribing to the capital stock of said company shall vote a written or printed ticket "for subscription," and those opposed shall so vote "against subscription," and each election shall be advertised and held under the same rules and regulations as are provided for the election of members of the general assembly.

SEC. 29. The bonds so issued shall be taken by said company at par.

SEC. 30. The board of justices of the peace for each township and their successors in office shall represent and vote said township stock at any regular or special meeting of said company.

SEC. 31. This act shall be in force from its ratification.

Ratified 5th day of March, A. D. 1879.

·

CHAPTER 131.—AN ACT

FOR THE BENEFIT OF THE WINSTON, SALEM AND MOORESVILLE RAILROAD COMPANY.

The General Assembly of North Carolina do enact:

SECTION 1. The board of directors of the penitentiary shall, on application of the chairman of the board of directors of said railroad company, or the president of said road, or an authorized agent, to employ on said road, under the direction of the authorities of said road, and under such guards as may be necessary, as many convicts as, in the opinion of the chairman of the board of. directors of said railroad company or the president of said road, as may be required, not to exceed one hundred and fifty; said convicts to be governed by and according to prison rules and regulations, and under the supervision and control of a superintendent appointed by and subject to the penitentiary board: *Provided, however,* that the authorities of the road upon which said convicts may work shall pay the hire of said superintendent, and guard, feed, clothe and properly care for said convicts while employed upon said road.

SEC. 2. The convicts obtained under this act shall be worked upon said road until the completion of the grading of said road.

SEC. 3. That the said chairman of the board of directors of [the Winston, Salem and Mooresville] railroad company, or the president of said road, shall before receiving the same from [the superintendent] or the directors of the penitentiary aforesaid, execute a receipt, stating the names of said convicts, the county where, and the offences of which, he was convicted, and the term of his sentence; and at the expiration of the sentence or the completion of the road the president of said road shall deliver the said convicts to the authorities of the penitentiary as the case may be.

SEC. 4. Nothing in this act contained shall be construed to interfere with, or take away any of the convicts assigned to any railroad in which the state has an interest.

SEC. 5. That this act shall be in force from and after its ratification.

Ratified the 6th day of March, A. D. 1879.

CHAPTER 137,—AN ACT

SUPPLEMENTARY TO AN ACT AUTHORIZING THE WORKING OF CONVICTS ON THE ORE KNOB AND MOUNT AIRY NARROW GAUGE RAILROAD, AND THE CHESTER AND LENOIR, AND THE CALDWELL AND WATAUGA NARROW GAUGE RAILROAD, AND THE WINSTON, MOORESVILLE AND SALEM RAILROAD, AND THE STATESVILLE AIR-LINE RAILROAD COMPANY, AND AUTHORIZING THE TRANSFER OF CONVICTS FROM ONE OF SAID RAILROAD COMPANIES TO THE OTHER.

The General Assembly of North Carolina do enact:

SECTION 1. That the president and directors of the Chester and Lenoir, and the Caldwell and Watauga Narrow Gauge Railroad Companies, the Winston, Mooresville and Salem Railroad, and the Statesville Air-Line Railroad Company, may, whenever they may find it to be their interest to do so, turn over all the convicts assigned to said railroad companies to one another for such time as may be agreed upon by the president and directors of said railroad companies, to be worked under the same rules, regulations and provisions as to the government, feeding, guarding, clothing, &c., as by law the convicts assigned to be worked on the Ore Knob and Mount Airy Narrow Gauge Railroad and the other companies are to be worked.

SEC. 2. That the president and directors of the Ore Knob and Mount Airy Narrow Gauge Railroad Company and each of the companies may in the same manner as provided for the transfer of convicts in section first of this act, transfer the convicts assigned by law to the Ore Knob and Mount Airy Narrow Gauge Railroad to the Chester and Lenoir and the Caldwell and Watauga Narrow Gauge Railroad Companies, or either of them, and all the convicts worked on the said Chester and Lenoir, or the Caldwell and Watauga Narrow Gauge Railroads, shall be worked upon the same terms and under the same rules, regulations and provisions as to the feeding, guarding, clothing, &c., as by law is provided for the working of convicts on the Ore Knob and Mount Airy Narrow Guage Railroad.

SEC. 3. The Chester and Lenoir and the Caldwell and Watauga Railroad, and the Ore Knob and Mount Airy Railroad, or either of them, may turn over the convicts hereby or heretofore granted to any or all of said roads, to the Cape Fear and Yadkin Valley Railroad, to be worked by said Cape Fear and Yadkin Valley Railroad under the same regulations and conditions as the convicts heretofore granted to the said Cape Fear and Yadkin Valley Railroad.

SEC. 4. All laws and clauses of laws coming in conflict with this act be and the same is hereby repealed.

Ratified the 7th day of March, A. D. 1879.

CHAPTER 243.—AN ACT

For the more speedy Procurement of the right of way by the Winston, Salem and Mooresville Railroad Company, and for the better Protection of Land-owners over whose lands said Railroad Passes.

The General Assembly of North Carolina do enact:

SECTION 1. That before the Winston, Salem and Mooresville Railroad Company shall enter upon the lands of any one over which they have located the track of said road for the purpose of constructing the same, and with whom they have failed to agree as to the amount of compensation for the right of way over said lands, it shall be lawful for the president or chairman of said railroad company to file a petition under oath before the clerk of the superior court of the county in which said lands are situated, setting forth the name of the party or parties interested in the lands sought to be condemned, with a description of the lands and a map of said line of railroad as located over said lands.

SEC. 2. That upon the filing of said petition by said railroad company the clerk of the court before whom said petition is filed shall issue a summons to the person or persons named in the petition to appear before him within twenty days after service of said summons on him or them and answer said petition; and on the coming in of the answer the said clerk shall issue a writ of venire to the sheriff of said county, commanding him to select the names of twenty-four good and lawful men from the vicinage of said lands qualified to act as jurors, from which number there shall be drawn, under the rules and regulations of drawing juries in the superior court, twelve men, which twelve men so drawn, after being duly sworn by the sheriff, shall assemble within five days at some place designated by the sheriff adjacent to the land or lands to be condemned, and with the sheriff or one of his deputies proceed upon the lands to be condemned and ascertain the actual damage done thereto by reason of the construction of said Winston, Salem and Mooresville Railroad, at the same time taking into consideration the benefit accruing to said lands by reason of the construction of said railroad and to deduct [the] same from said amount of damage; but in no case shall the benefits be considered to exceed the value of said lands and a judgment be given therefor against any party or parties over whose lands said road passes. Either party to such proceedings may have the right of appeal; and if any assessment is made against said railroad company, by said amount being paid into the superior court clerk's office said railroad may enter upon said lands and prosecute its work.

SEC. 3. All laws and clauses of laws in conflict with this act are hereby repealed.

SEC. 4. That this act shall be in force from and after its ratification.

Ratified the 14th day of March, A. D. 1879.

_____

CHAPTER 109.—AN ACT

To incorporate the Dan Valley and Yadkin River Narrow Gauge Railroad Company.

The General Assembly of North Carolina do enact:

SECTION 1. That it shall be lawful for the Dan Valley and Yadkin River Narrow Gauge Railroad Company, a corporation created by and under the laws of the state of Virginia, passed for that purpose, and approved January twenty-second, one thosand eight hundred and seventy-nine, to extend, construct and operate a railroad from the Virginia state line, on the border of Rockingham county in this state, in the vicinity of Leaksville, to connect with its road in Virginia when completed, through the counties of Rockingham, Stokes, Forsyth, Yadkin, Surry, and Wilkes, or either of them, and such other counties as may be deemed necessary by said company, to reach the most desirable points for such railroad or the most desirable connection with any other railroad in this state: and for this purpose the said company shall have, use and enjoy, in this state, all the rights, franchise and privileges, which other corporate bodies may lawfully exercise under chapter ninety-nine (99), Battle's Revisal, page seven hundred and twenty-seven, entitled railroad companies, or which were granted the North Carolina Railroad Company under its act act of incorporation, or the several acts amendatory thereof: and shall have the exclusive right of conveyance or transportation of persons and things over their said railroad when constructed at such charges as may be fixed by them: *Provided*, That nothing herein contained shall be construed so as to exempt from taxation any of the property or franchises of said company.

SEC. 2. It shall be lawful to secure subscription to the capital stock of said company in money, labor, land or materials, such as timber, stone, lumber, or supplies of any kind usually required in the construction of a railroad; and it shall also be lawful to receive the bonds of any city, town, county or township in payment of subscription, and the said company may also acquire land by gift or purchase, and shall have power to hold and sell the same for construction or repair of their said road, for depots, or other necessary purposes.

SEC. 3. That said company shall have power to build branch or lateral roads, not exceeding fifty miles in length, to connect with any mines, iron works or other manufactories.

SEC. 4. Subscriptions to the capital stock of this company may be made by individuals, by any city, town. county or township, and by any railroad company, or any mining or manufacturing company.

SEC. 5. It shall be lawful for said railroad company to borrow money for the construction, maintenance and repair of its road or any branch thereof, and also to issue bonds, and secure the same by mortgaging its property and franchises or otherwise.

SEC. 6. It shall be lawful for said company to lease out its road, property, rights and franchises to individuals or to any other company or corporations, also to lease the road, property, rights and franchises of any other company connecting with said company's road: also to consolidate its stock and property with that of any other company connecting with it, whether chartered by this or any other state: also to make any contract or agreement by which the road-bed and rolling stock of said company or any part thereof may be constructed and used in whole or in part, by the Danville and New River Narrow Gauge Railroad Company, or any other whole line of railroad shall connect with said company's road.

SEC. 7. Whenever the company and the landowners cannot agree for the use of land along the line of the company's road, commissioners shall be appointed as provided for by law, to ascertain the value of the same; said commissioners so appointed shall on ascertaining the damages, take into consideration the advantages and benefits to accrue to such landowner by the construction of said road through his or her land.

SEC. 8. This act shall be in force from and after its ratification.

In the general assembly read three times, and ratified this the 19th day of February, A. D. 1881.

CHAPTER 162.—AN ACT

To Authorize the North-Western North Carolina Railroad Company to extend its Road
and to Build Branches Thereof.

The General Assembly of North Carolina do enact:

SECTION 1. That it shall be lawful for the North-western
North Carolina railroad company to extend and construct
its line of road, or a branch thereof, to commence at or
near Winston in the county of Forsyth, through the counties of Forsyth, Davidson, Yadkin, Davie, Rowan and Iredell, or any or either of them, to Statesville or some other
point on the Western North Carolina railroad, and may
build and operate additional branches thereto, or from
its present main line to any important mines or manfac-
tories in any of said counties, or counties adjacent to
them: Provided, That nothing contained in this act shall
operate or be construed so as to prevent or interfere with
the construction of the North Carolina extension of the
Virginia Midland railroad from Danville, Virginia, via
Winston, Forsyth county, and Mocksville, Davie county,
to some point on the Atlantic, Tennessee and Ohio railroad in Iredell county; but said company is hereby authorized to build said road under the organization and
consolidation heretofore made by the stockholders and
directors of the consolidated line composing the North
Carolina extension.

SEC. 2. That to provide the means in whole or in part
for this purpose, the said company may receive subscriptions in money, labor, property or otherwise, as the said
company may agree, and may mortgage or otherwise
pledge its property and franchises and the work constructed, or to be constructed, with the franchises and
rights connected therewith.

SEC. 3. That any corporation, county, city, town or

township interested therein, may subs .il e to stock for said purpo_e or otheiwi.e contribute 'o such work in such manner and in such amount as shall be determined by the proper authorities of such corporation, county, city, town or township, and agreed on with the said Northwestern North Carolina railroad company.

SEC. 4. This act shall be in force from and after its ratification.

In the general assembly read three times, and ratified this the 2nd day of March, A. D. 1881.

CHAPTER 205.—AN ACT
To Secure the Completion of the North Carolina Midland Railroad.

The General Assembly of North Carolina do enact:

SECTION 1. That the stockholders of the North Carolina Midland Railroad Company, resident in this State, shall have power, in a meeting of such stockholders to be called as hereinafter provided, to rescind any action by which they have heretofore accepted any subscription from the Virginia Midland Railroad Company, or other parties non-resident in North Carolina: *Provided*, that the North Carolina Midland Railroad Company shall adjust any claims against it held by the Virginia Midland Railroad Company or other parties, in accordance with the conditions of contracts heretofore existing.

SEC. 2. That upon request of stockholders owning and representing one-fourth of the stock held in North Carolina, it shall be the duty of the vice-president of the North Carolina Midland Railroad Company, resident in the State, to call a meeting of all the stockholders residing in this State, notice having been issued to each stockholder in accordance with the rules of the company.

SEC. 3. The North Carolina Midland Railroad Company

is hereby authorized to call upon the penitentiary authorities for one hundred and fifty convicts, not otherwise appropriated, to be paid for at the rate of one hundred and twenty-five dollars each per year, in cash or bonds of the counties, townships, cities and towns along the line of said railroad.

SEC. 4. That this act shall be in force from and after its ratification.

In the General Assembly read three times, and ratified this the 4th day of March, A. D. 1885.

CHAPTER 99.—BATTLE'S REVISAL.

58. It shall and may be lawful for any railroad company or other corporation, organized under the laws of this State, or of this State and any other State, and operating a railroad or bridge either wholly within or partly within and partly without this State, to merge and consolidate its capital stock, franchises and property with the capital stock, franchises and property of any other railroad company or companies organized under the laws of this State, or under the laws of this State and any other State, or under the laws of any other State or States, whenever the two or more railroads of the companies or corporation so to be consolidated shall or may form a continuous line of railroad with each other or by means of any intervening railroad, bridge or ferry.

59. Said consolidation shall be made under the conditions, provisions and restrictions, and with the powers hereafter in this chapter mentioned and contained, that is to say:

(1.) The directors of the companies proposing to consolidate may enter into a joint agreement under the corporate seal of each company for the consolidation of said companies and railroads, and prescribing the terms and conditions thereof, the mode of carrying the same into effect, the name of the new corperation, the number and names of the directors and other officers thereof, and who shall be the first directors and officers, and their places of residence, the number of shares of the capital stock, the amount or par value of each share, and the manner of converting the capital stock of each of the said companies into that of the new corporation, and how and when directors and officers shall be chosen, with such other details as they shall deem necessary to perfect such new organization and the consolidation of said companies or railroads.

(2.) Said agreement shall be submitted to the stockholders of each of the said companies or corporations at a meeting thereof called separately for the purpose of taking the same into consideration; due notice of the time and place of holding said meeting, and object thereof, shall be given by each company to its stockholders by written or printed notices, addressed to each of the persons in whose names the capital stock of such company stands on the books thereof, and delivered to such persons respectively or sent to them by mail when their postoffice address is known to the company, at least thirty days before the time of holding such meeting, and also by a general notice, published daily for at least four weeks in some newspaper printed in the city, town or county where such company has its principal office or place of business ; and at the said meeting of stockholders the agreement of the said directors shall be considered and a vote by ballot taken for the adoption or rejection of the same, each share entitling the holder thereof to one vote, and said ballots shall be cast in person or by proxy, and if two-thirds of all the votes of all the stockholders shaal be for the adoption of said agreement, then that fact shall be certified thereon by the secretaries of the respective companies nnder seals thereof, and the agreement so adopted, or a certified copy thereof, shall be filed in the office of the Secretary of State, and shall from thence be deemed and taken to be the agreement and act of consolidation of the said companies; and a copy of the said agreement and act of consolidation, duly certified by the Secretary of State under his official seal, shall be evidence in all courts and places of the existence of said new corporation, and that the foregoing provisions of this chapter have been fully observed and complied with.

60. Upon the making and perfecting of such agreement and act of consolidation as hereinbefore provided, and filing the same or a copy thereof in the office of the Secretary of State as aforesaid, the said corporations, parties thereto, shall be deemed and taken to be one corporation by the name provided in said agreement and act, but such act of consolidation shall not release such new corporations from any of the restrictions, liabilities or duties of the several corporations so consolidated.

61. Upon the consummation of said act of consolidation as aforesaid, all and singnlar the rights, privileges, exemptions and franchises of each of said corporations, parties to the same, and all the property, real, personal and mixed, and all debts due on whatever account to either of said corporations as well as all stock subscriptions and other things in action belonging to either of said corporations shall be taken and deemed to be transferred to and vested in such new corporation without further act or deed; and all claims, demands, property, rights of way and every other interest, shall be as effectuaily the property of the new corporation as they were of the former corporations, parties to the said agreement and act, and the title to all real estate taken by deed or otherwise, under the laws of this State vested in either of such corporations, parties to said agreement and act,

shall not be deemed to revert or be in any way impaired by reason of this chapter or anything done by virtue thereof, but shall be vested in the new corporation by virtue of such act of consolidation.

62. The rights of all creditors and all liens upon the property of either of said corporations, parties to said agreement and act, shall be preserved unimpaired, and the respective corporations shall be deemed to continue in existence to preserve the same; and all debts and liabilities incurred by either of said corporations except mortgages, shall thenceforth attach to such new corporation and be enforced against it and its property to the same extent as if said debts or liabilities had been incurred or contracted by it. No suit, action or other proceeding pending before any court or tribunal in which either of said railroad companies is a party shall be deemed to have abated or been discontinued by the agreement and act of consolidation as aforesaid, but the same may be conducted in the name of the existing corporation to final judgment, or such new corporation may be, by order of the court, on motion, substituted as a party. Suits may be brought and maintained against such new corporation in the courts of this State for all causes of action in the same manner as against other railroad corporations therein.